My partner doe dogs.
What would my dog say?

I'm taking too many
pictures of him.
What would my dog say?

I'm eating a lot.
What would my dog say?

I think I'm getting fat.
What would my dog say?

There's cat food in the house.
What would my dog say?

I'm ignoring him.
What would my dog say?

I don't bother combing him.
What would my dog say?

I've been wearing the same shirt for three days.
What would my dog say?

I've got a date.
What would my dog say?

I'm hungry again.
What would my dog say?

I still haven't fed him.
What would my dog say?

I haven't taken a bath.
What would my dog say?

I snore.
What would my dog say?

I tasted dog food and nearly threw up.
What would my dog say?

M dog runs faster than me.
What would my dog say?

I'm too busy to pet him.
What would my dog say?

I'm telling my friends that dogs are better than cats. *What would my dog say?*

I haven't gotten out of the house for a while.
What would my dog say?

I'm making funny faces in front of the mirror.
What would my dog say?

I'm checking someone out.
What would my dog say?

I'm eating with my hands.
What would my dog say?

I'm having my sixth cup of coffee for the day.
What would my dog say?

I've been eating all day and have forgotten to feed her. *What would my dog say?*

I'm too heavy and yet I insist on putting my leg on top of him.
What would my dog say?

I'm too lazy to walk him.
What would my dog say?

We're both staring at that last slice of pizza.
What would my dog say?

I forced him to wear a t-shirt.
What would my dog say?

I kept saying I'm too fat.
What would my dog say?

It's raining.
What would my dog say?

I brought someone home.
What would my dog say?

I'm wearing a suit.
What would my dog say?

I got another dog.
What would my dog say?

I'm drunk.
What would my dog say?

(Create your own scenario.)
What would my dog say?

What would my dog say?

What would my dog say?

What would my dog say?

What would my dog say?

What would my dog say?

What would my dog say?

What would my dog say?

What would my dog say?

What would my dog say?

What would my dog say?

What would my dog say?

What would my dog say?

What would my dog say?

What would my dog say?

What would my dog say?

Printed in Great Britain
by Amazon

WHAT WOULD WOULD MY DOG SAY?

A guess on what Dogs Really think of Humans